LITTLE QUOTES BY LITTLE FOLKS

A COLLECTION OF FUNNY, PROFOUND AND JUST PLAIN ABSURD QUOTES FROM KIDS AROUND THE WORLD.

ILLUSTRATED BY JAKE OLSON
EDITED BY REBECCA CARTER, TIA LEVINGS
AND SARAH WEBSTER PLITT

Little Quotes by Little Folks

Published by Rebecca Carter
Miami, Florida

Illustrated by Jake Olson
Edited by Rebecca Carter, Tia Levings, Sarah Webster Plitt

ISBN: 978-0-578-73397-5

Visit LittleQuotesBook.com for more information or to submit a quote.
Email info@littlequotesbook.com to contact us or for bulk purchases.

OUR KIDS SAY SOME OF
THE MOST PROFOUND, FUNNY AND
JUST PLAIN ABSURD THINGS-
AND WE KNOW YOURS DO TOO!

LITTLE QUOTES BY LITTLE FOLKS
IS A COLLABORATIVE BOOK PROJECT
MADE WITH CONTRIBUTIONS FROM
KIDS AROUND THE WORLD.

I Like your
PLANTS

BUT I CAN TELL
THAT THEY'RE FAKE.

OLIVIA   AGE 6

IF CATS COULD FLY...
THAT WOULD BE
THE END
OF THE BIRDS
WOULDN'T IT?

NATHANIEL   AGE 8

MOM : WHAT DO YOU WANT FOR DINNER?

RORY :

NOTHING.

FOOD GIVES ME

⚡ **ENERGY** ⚡

AND I HAVE **PLENTY**

OF **THAT**, MOMMY!

RORY   AGE 5

DAD: DID YOU ASK ME SOMETHING?

ALANA: I WAS TALKING TO <u>MY</u> <u>SANDWICH</u>.

ALANA   AGE 15

DYLAN: LADIES FIRST.

MOM: THANK YOU!

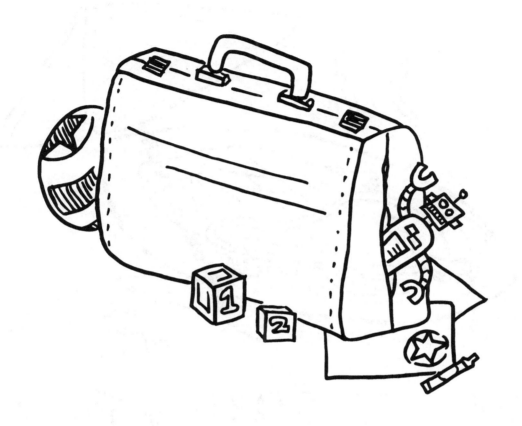

DYLAN: I'M WORKING ON
MY GROWN-UP STUFF.

DYLAN   AGE 7

WE ARE STARTING TO
ROAST LIKE BEEF!

ABBY   AGE 5

THIS DONUT IS SO YUMMY-

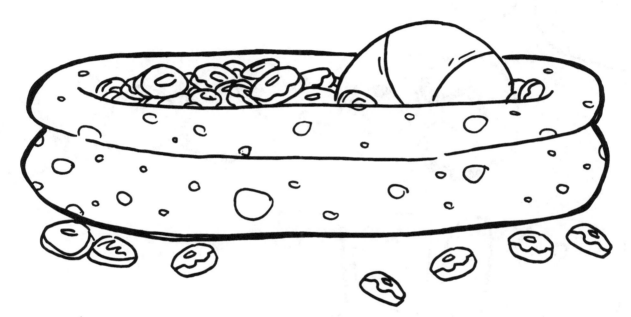

I WISH I COULD SWIM IN A POOL OF DONUTS.

JULIAN   AGE 5

DO COWBOYS RIDE COWS?

BLAKE   AGE 4

RORY: WHEN I WAS A BABY YOU BABYSAT ME BUT NOW I'M A KID SO YOU KIDSAT ME.

MOM: I'M YOUR PARENT SO I PARENT YOU.

DANNY: WHY DO YOU MAKE ME WEAR STUPID CLOTHES?

MOM: YOUR CLOTHES ARE NOT STUPID.

DANNY: A BEAR... FLYING AN AIRPLANE..?

DANNY   AGE 3

WHAT IF ALL MY TEETH FELL OUT AT THE
SAME TIME AND I PUT THEM UNDER MY PILLOW?
THE TOOTH FAIRY WOULD BE SO SURPRISED!

JULIAN   AGE 5

WHEN THE FIRE ALARM GOES OFF, THE BACON IS READY.

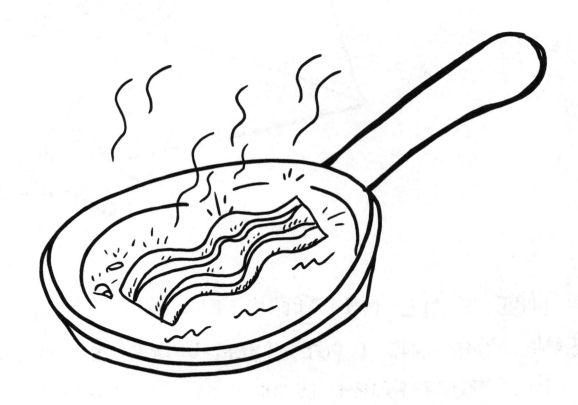

ALEX   AGE 6

I BURPED
SO THAT MEANS
I'M FINISHED.

OLIVER   AGE 4

MOM: JUST GIVE MOMMY ONE SECOND.

HUNTER: OK.

HUNTER   AGE 7

JOE   AGE 4

ALEC: WHAT'S THE LONGEST WORD YOU CAN SAY?

MAMI: SUPERCALIFRAGILISTIC EXPIALIDOCIOUS.

ALEC: MINE IS —

GOOOOOOOO

ALEC   AGE 9

HANNAH   AGE 2

CAN I HAVE A BOWL
OF CORN FLAGS?

ANNA JO   AGE 3

~~EYEBALL~~

"EYE BOB"

ALEC   AGE 3

~~SECURITY~~
~~GUARD~~

"CEREAL
GUARD"

FRANCESCO   AGE 3

BRYAN   AGE 4

DAD :

HOW ABOUT IF WE GO TO A
MUSEUM? DOES THAT SOUND GOOD?

JT:

YES! I WANNA GO! CAN WE GO
TO THE ANIMAL MUSEUM?!?!

DAD :

NO, AND IT'S CALLED A ZOO.

JT AGE 7

DYLAN: CAN I VIDEO CHAT WITH MY FRIEND?

MOM: SURE, BUT REMEMBER YOU NEED TO READ FROM 8:00 TO 9:00.

DYLAN: SURE, BUT CAN I READ TO MY FRIEND ON VIDEO CHAT?

DYLAN   AGE 9

MY NAME IS PENNY EXCEPT WHEN I'M NAUGHTY AND THEN IT'S PENELOPE.

PENNY   AGE 3 ¾

MOM: I HAVE TO GO TO MY FRIEND'S BABY SHOWER TODAY.

BLAKE: DO YOU HAVE TO GO NAKED?

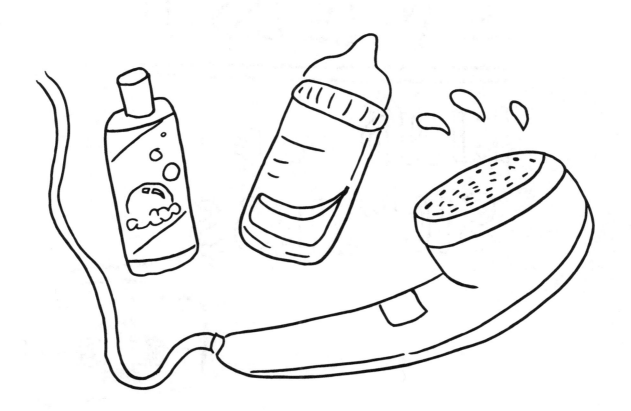

BLAKE   AGE 4

I HAVE EVERY
─────────
KIND OF
SICKNESS

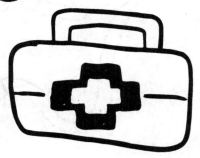

EXCEPT FOR

THE 'ILL' PART...

ANDREW   AGE 5

MOM: WE ARE FLYING HOME TO MIAMI.

TARYN: IT'S NOT "YOUR-AMI"
IT'S "MY-AMI"!

TARYN   AGE 3½

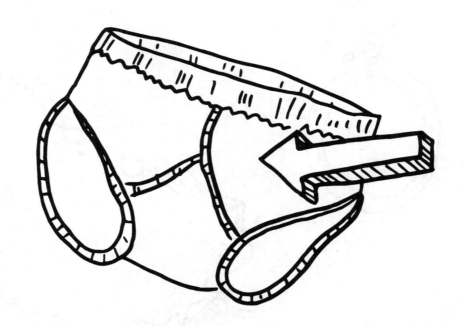

PHILIP   AGE 3

MOM: WHAT ARE YOU DOING?

AUBREY: JUST SITTING ON MY NUTS.

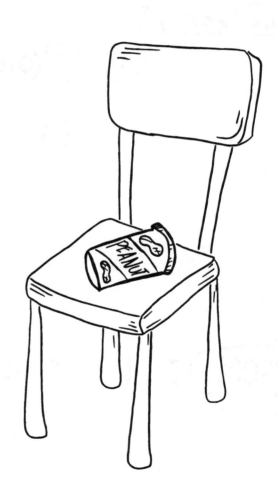

AUBREY   AGE 2

OLIVER : I POOPED TODAY! I WIN!

MOM : THERE IS NO WINNING IN POOPING.

OLIVER : IF THERE WAS WINNING THOUGH-
I WOULD WIN.

OLIVER   AGE 4

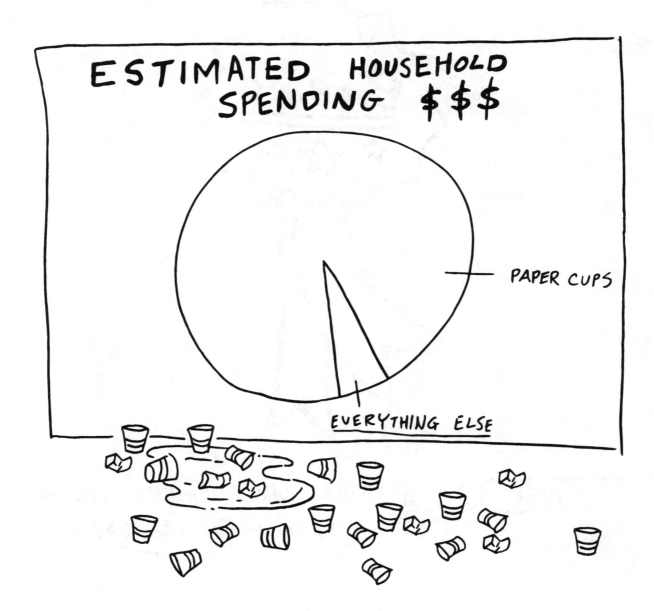

MOM: STOP WASTING PAPER CUPS!

STEVEN:

THAT'S OKAY,

DADDY

CAN BUY THEM!

STEVEN AGE 3

OH NO, MY PRE-PRENDIX IS COMING OUT!

CELIA   AGE 4

DAD:

Do you know what "difficult" means?

KELAN:

...No

KELAN   AGE 5

WHERE CAN I FIND SPONSORBILITY? MOM SAID I NEED THAT TO GET A DOG.

FELICITY   AGE 4

NOW MY TABLET
SMELLS LIKE
FARTS
BECAUSE YOU PUT
HOT DOGS ON IT.

GIAVANNA   AGE 5

TOO BAD WE CAN'T GO TO THE PLACE I FORGOT THE NAME OF ANYMORE.

AIDEN   AGE 5

DADDY, YOU SHOULD BE A DOCTOR
WHEN YOU GROW UP
SO YOU CAN TAKE CARE OF ME.

ANNORA   AGE 6

MOM: GIVE ME THE LAST NAMES OF THESE PRESIDENTS: GEORGE —

NICOLAS: WASHINGTON

MOM: ABRAHAM —

NICOLAS: LINCOLN

MOM: BARACK —

NICOLAS: OBAMA

MOM : TEDDY -

NICOLAS : BEAR!

NICOLAS   AGE 7

YOU'RE A BAD MOMMY!

I'M GOING TO THROW YOU
IN THE TRASH!

SANTINO   AGE 3½

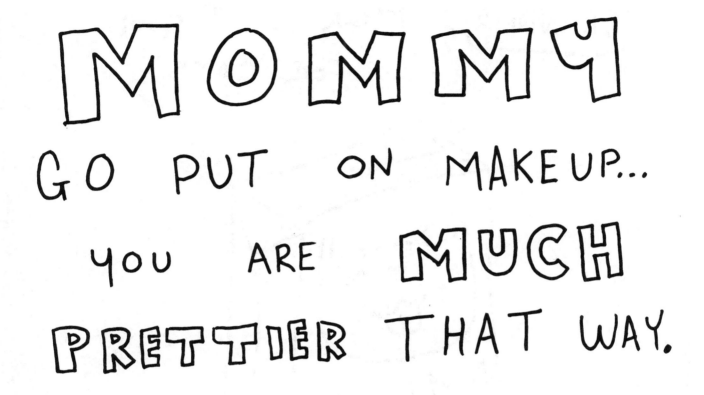

MOMMY
GO PUT ON MAKEUP...
YOU ARE MUCH
PRETTIER THAT WAY.

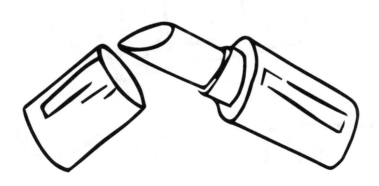

PAISLEY   AGE 7

GRANDMA : MILK ISN'T GOOD
FOR CATS.

OLIVER : CAT MILK IS.

OLIVER   AGE 5

DO YOU WANT TO TRY MY NUT SNACK?

OLIVIA   AGE 2

I LOVE BEING 4 BECAUSE NOW I KNOW EVERYTHING.

JOE   AGE 4

FOR SUCH A LOW ME, THAT WAS SUCH A HIGH THROW!

RORY   AGE 4½

MAMI, I LOVE THE MOON!
WHEN I GROW UP, I AM GOING
TO BE A WEREWOLF!

ANDREAS   AGE 3

LOOK MOMMY, THAT CAR HAS HIS FLASHLIGHTS ON!

JAX   AGE 4

HANNAH   AGE 2

THEY'RE CALLED THE SMOKY MOUNTAINS
BECAUSE THEY ARE ALL
VOLCANOES.

GRANT   AGE 6

AILA: DADDY, WHAT DO YOU WANT?

DADDY: I WANT A DAUGHTER WHO LISTENS
AND RESPECTS HER PARENTS.

AILA: <u>SORRY</u>, WE DON'T HAVE THAT.

AILA   AGE 4

I LIKE THIS STORE, THEY GIVE OUT

EXAMPLES !

KADE   AGE 6

BO   AGE 4

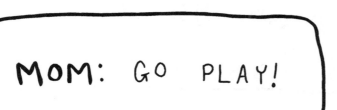

MAUREEN   AGE 11

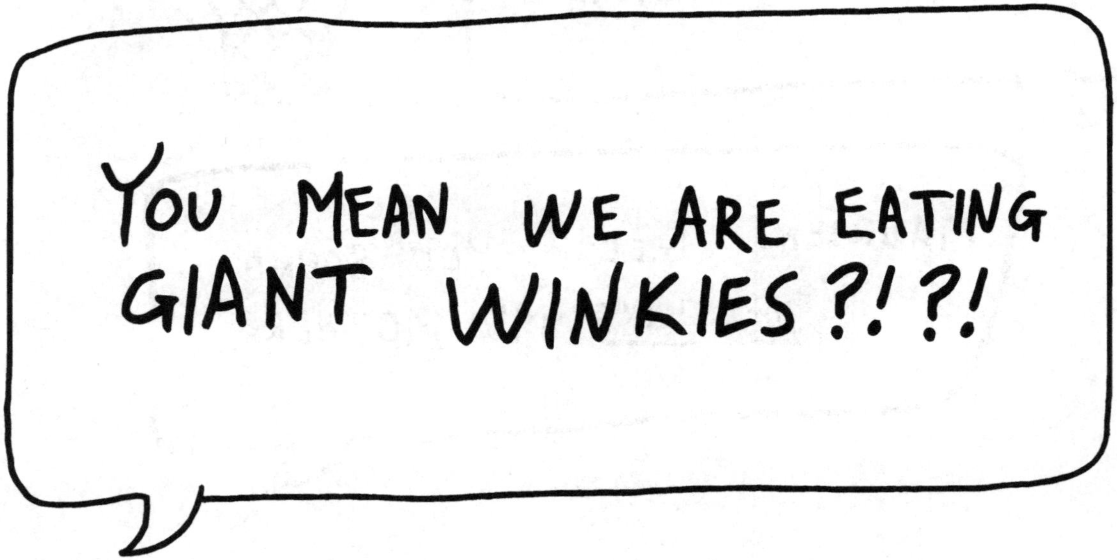
YOU MEAN WE ARE EATING GIANT WINKIES ?! ?!

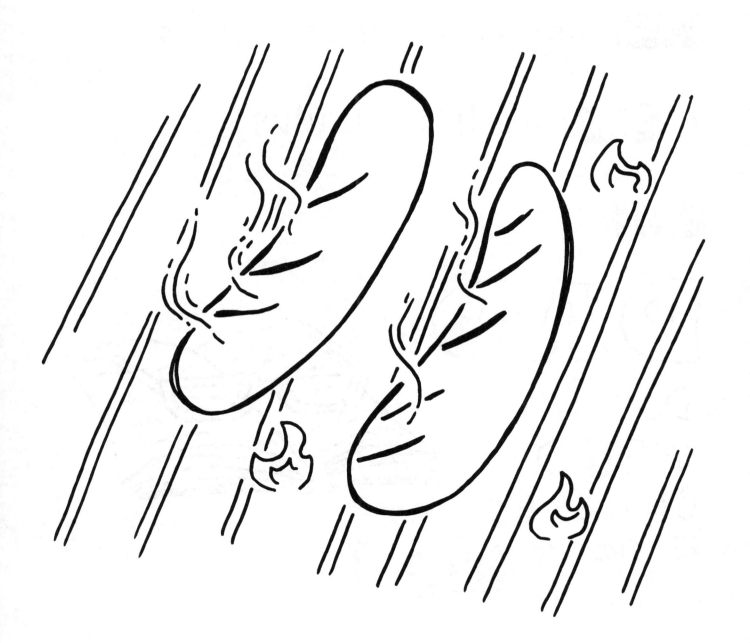

WHEATON   AGE 6

MOMMY, I REALLY REALLY LIKE SUGAR.
THAT'S MY FAVORITE FOOD.

JAMES   AGE 3

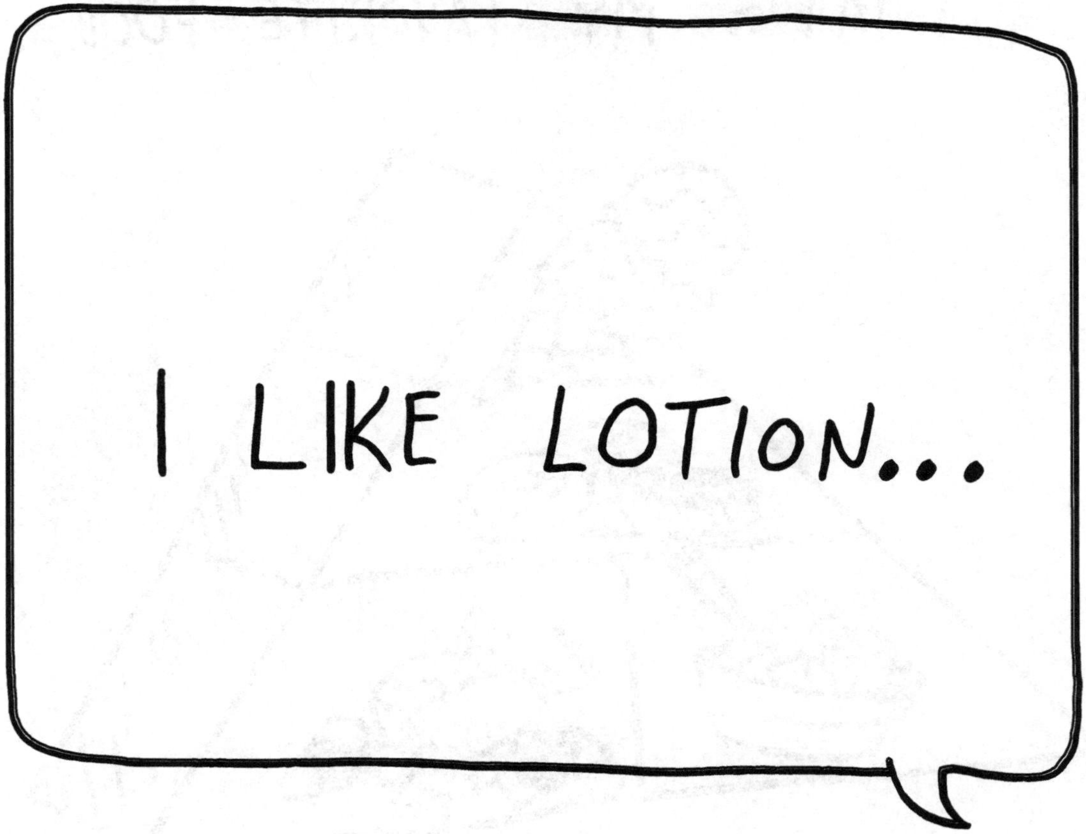
I LIKE LOTION...

...IT TASTES LIKE SOAP.

REMINGTON   AGE 2½

I'M NOT A LAZY PERSON BUT I JUST NEED A

LAZY:DAY

DYLAN   AGE 9

MOMMY! MY FART'S
ON THE FLOOR!

AILA   AGE 4

MOM: SORRY I RAISED MY VOICE TODAY.

ARALYN: IT'S OK, YOU ARE A REALLY GOOD YELLER...

...YOU COULD SCARE AWAY MONSTERS
YOU ARE SO LOUD!

ARALYN   AGE 4

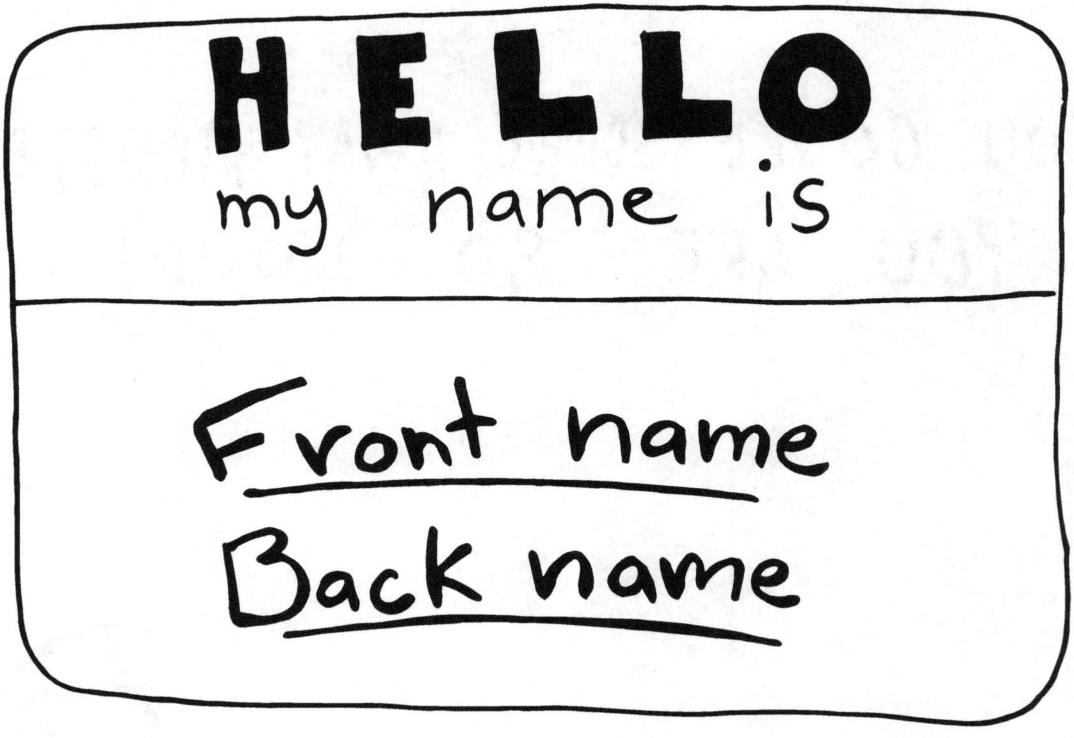

WHAT'S MY FRONT NAME AND BACK NAME?

ILA AGE 3

MOMMY, THAT LADY IS SHRIVELED UP
LIKE AN OLD PRUNE.

SARAH   AGE 2

PAPI,

HOW DO LADYBUGS

DEFEND THEIRSELVES?

OLIVER AGE 5

RORY   AGE 3½

ONLY LOVE
    LASTS FOREVER...
            AND DIRT.

XAVIER   AGE 7

MY EYES WERE DRIPPING
WHEN YOU WERE GONE.

VIANNA   AGE 3½

I'M GONNA BE IN
THE FUTURE
SO <u>WATCH</u> <u>OUT</u>!

ALANA   AGE 11

MOM: HANNAH, WHAT DO YOU WANT
TO BE WHEN YOU GROW UP?

HANNAH: A DOCTOR.

MOM: OH YEAH? DO YOU WANT TO TAKE CARE
OF BABIES OR GROWN-UPS?

HANNAH: DINOSAURS!

HANNAH   AGE 2

I'M NOT TIRED

MY EYES ARE MAKING MY FACE FALL ASLEEP.

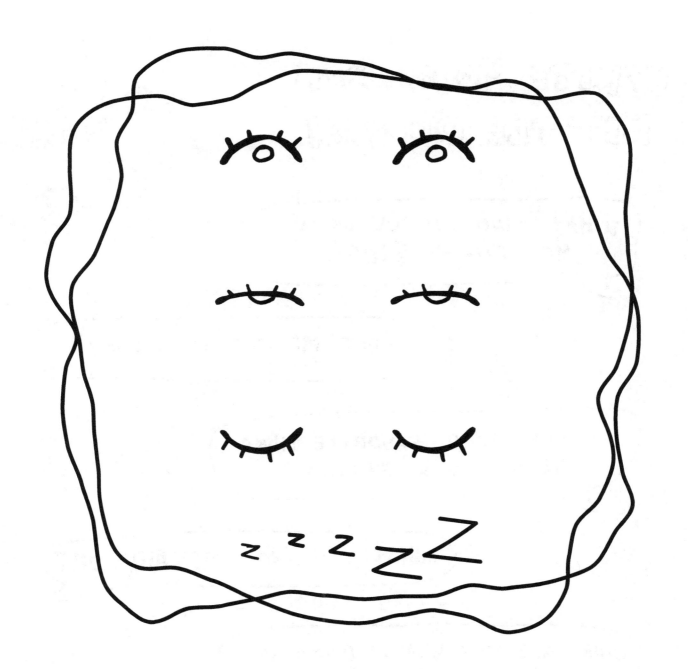

ANNA   AGE 4

WRITE YOUR OWN LITTLE QUOTES!

HERE ARE SOME QUESTIONS TO GET YOU STARTED!

WHAT WOULD YOU DO IF YOU FOUND $100?

WHAT MAKES YOU LAUGH?

WHAT'S YOUR FAVORITE THING ABOUT OUR FAMILY?

WHAT ARE YOU AFRAID OF?

WHAT ARE YOU REALLY GOOD AT?

WOULD YOU RATHER BE A GROWN-UP OR A KID?

HAVE YOU EVER TOLD A LIE?

WHAT ARE YOUR PARENTS' JOBS?

HOW BIG IS THE WORLD?

IF YOU COULD CHOOSE YOUR OWN NAME, WHAT WOULD IT BE?

WRITE YOUR OWN LITTLE QUOTES!

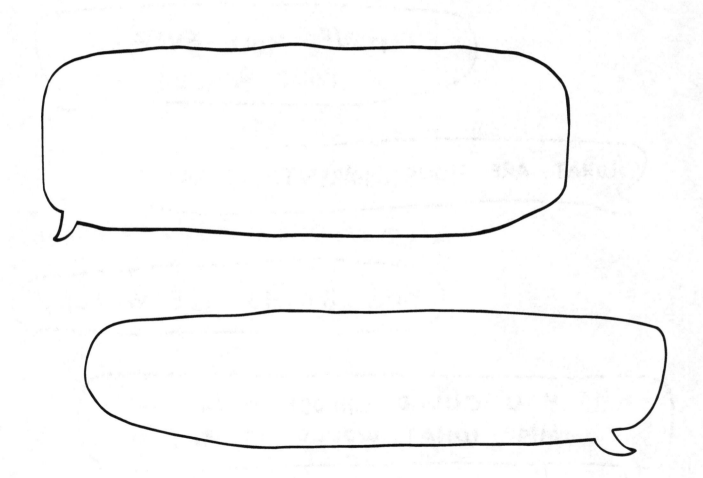

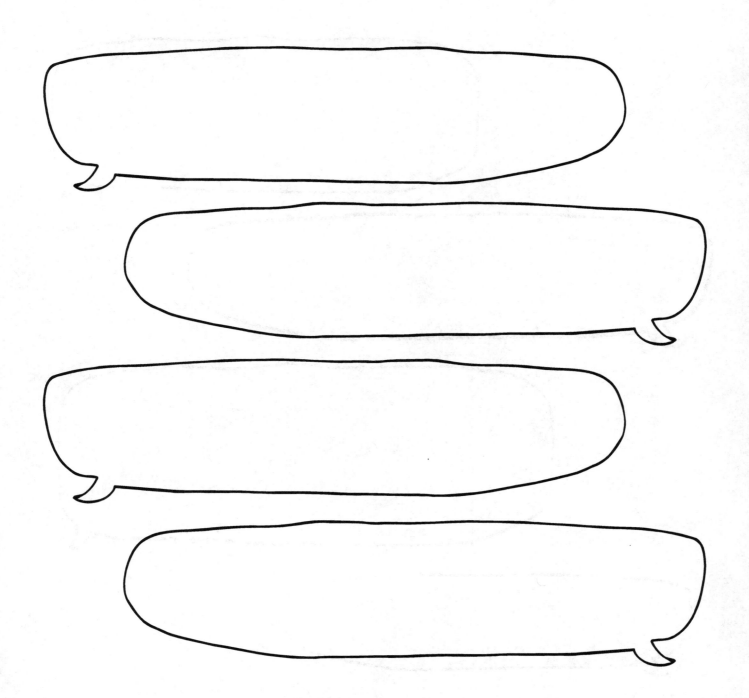

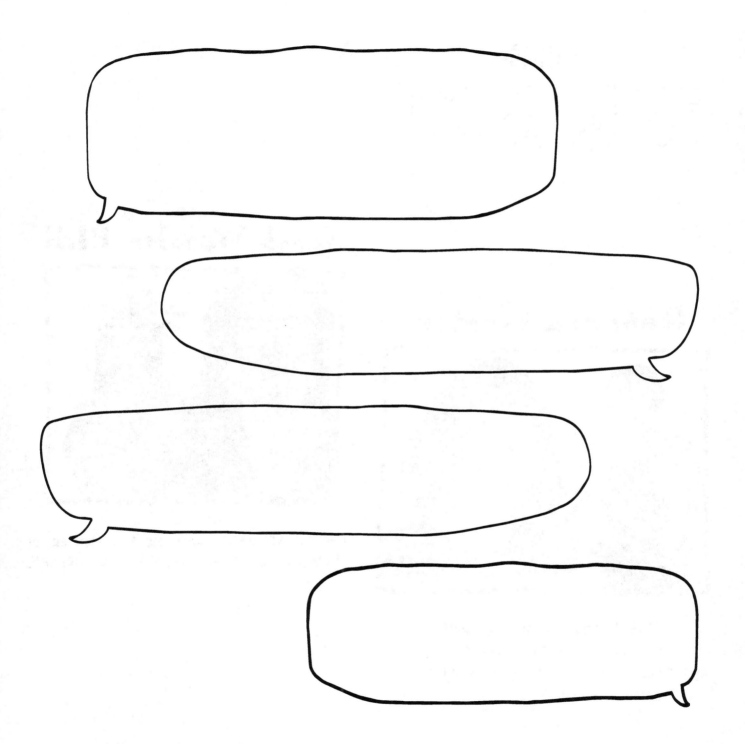

THE TEAM

Rebecca Carter

I'M A MOTHER OF TWO BOYS,
COLLABORATIVE ARTIST
AND FREELANCE CONSULTANT IN MIAMI, FLORIDA.

Sarah Webster Plitt

I'M AN ACTRESS, WRITER AND MOTHER OF
TWO LITTLE PRINCESSES IN NEW JERSEY.

Tia Levings

I'M A MOM TO KIDS AND DOGS, A WRITER, ARTIST AND MAKER IN JACKSONVILLE, FLORIDA.

Jake Olson

I'M A FREELANCE DESIGNER AND ILLUSTRATOR WORKING IN WESTERN NEW YORK.

A HUGE
THANK YOU

TO OUR CROWDFUNDING BACKERS!

COLLABORATING WITH YOU HAS BEEN A DREAM COME TRUE.

ANNIE CARTER
THE LANG FAMILY
THE HUTCHINSON FAMILY
MATT "JTFK" HALEY-JOHNSTON
FERDI RODRIGUEZ
BREI O'FEE

THE WEBSTER FAMILY
THE ANGULO FAMILY
THE DeWITT/HARRIS FAMILY
THE MARTINEZ FAMILY
THE PALACIO GUERRERO FAMILY
THE MUSSELMAN FAMILY

THE O'CONNELL FAMILY
KAITLIN, JON, AND HANNAH TRAINOR
THOM CRAIGEN
BETHANY MILLER
TIFFANY MARRIOTT
DEIRDRE HUGHES

PATRICK McCONNELL
THE BRAVO FAMILY
JOSEPH SLOTNICK
JAN SHAPIRO
THE PICERNO FAMILY (SANTINO, FRANCESCO,
JENNIE AND ANGELO)

9 780578 733975